KARMIC CHANTING

KARMIC CHANTING

Sonnet Mondal

copper coin

coppercoin

First published in India in 2018 by
Copper Coin Publishing Pvt Ltd
L5/903 Gulmohur Garden
Raj Nagar Extension
Ghaziabad 201017
Delhi NCR

www.coppercoin.co.in

Karmic Chanting

Cover painting: Brian Shileds
Cover design: Ritesh Kumar

ISBN 978-93-84109-32-5

Typeset by JMD Publisher Services, Patna
Printed and bound at Thomson Press (India) Ltd

The coming seconds will be gone soon

flowers about to bloom would fall
growing trees would succumb to time
rolling stones would turn into soil

if you have to cry   cry soon
if you have to laugh   laugh soon

the chords of sentiments too   will pass
raptures will be entombed by time

what would remain is   the remains

everything we sense
is not everything

Contents

Foreword	xiii
From Tushar's Apartment	1
The Lost Mango Tree	3
Strange Meetings	4
If I Could	5
###	6
Aperture	7
###	8
Masked Eyes	9
Grandma	10
Why	11
Answer Me, Ma	12
Slavery of Flags	14
Beginnings	15
Birth of a Hill	16
Locked	17

Being Yourself 18
Left-Out Love 19
Hunted 20
Barely Known 21
Blame 22
Journeying 23
Who Am I? 24
When I Hide 25
Freedom of Love 26
Cigarette Smoke 27
When the Wilderness Spoke 28
Like a Brick in a Wall 29
The Ferry's Night Horn 30
With Time 31
On a Moonlit Night 32
Parallels 33
Differences 34
In a Desert 35
Many Faces 36
Negating the Known 37
In Front of a Burning Corpse 38
Intentions 40
Tonguing Ashes 41
I Never Had a Favourite Face 42

The Air Around Me 44
Reaping the Need to Know 46
No One to Wait at the Doorstep 47
Through the Broken Window 48
The Rooftop 49
Dadaji 50
Through the Specs of an Old Man 52
Some Things Are Best Unchanged 54
April and My Plastic Sunflowers 55
My Chained Faith 56
Inception or Epilogue? 58
We Deserve a Jungle 60
A Duck's Life 61
Looking at Lake Ohrid 62
Afloat in Darkness 64
Teach Me 65
Liberty of Half-Dead Creations 66
Stories Told by Dimness 68
The Homeless 69
Talaq Talaq Talaq *70*
Tears 72
Nobody Speaks of You, Syria 73
The Soldier in the Moss 75
Snapshots of a Dying Soldier 76

To Syrian Children 78
Death of a Dalit 80
The Ragpicker 81
Faith in Times of War 82
Haze and High 83
Anticipations Grip Back 84
Untitled 85
Smells 86
Asides 87

Foreword

Followers of contemporary poetry who've heard Sonnet Mondal reading his poems at international festivals will know something of the distinctiveness of his voice and the philosophising delicacy of his work. In *Karmic Chanting* he has assembled many of his most beautiful recent poems. His is a poetry of light and shadow, of shimmering childhood and reflective adulthood: 'My mind is heavier than my soul,' he writes, and 'I wish I had left myself / to the charity of wilderness.' Here we find something of the tension between inner and outer worlds—and the way one betrays the other—as well as the remembered pain of such perceptions. Here is the poet 'as a meditating owl / hooting mantras in the zero hour.' His is a poetry of brilliant metaphors and similes, such as the sight of flags on their flag-poles 'like fish / trapped by fish hooks' or the human life lived by daylight assembled for the night as a heap of broken mirrors. A poet of both wilderness and solitude, he speaks to us of the sovereignty of love, of the elasticity and nebulousness of time, but also of the precise knowledge gained at the end of things as he watches a corpse burning 'in the burning ghat by the sea.' As he says, so accurately, it's not that he's had a favourite face but a favourite perception. Whether he's thinking of the WhatsApp selfie taken in a glassy arcade in Dubai or the four plastic sunflowers in his bedroom (a harvest from a toxic April in his life), he remains, at all times, the philosopher-poet, the one creating a balancing act between being and non-being. Here, then, is a poetic voice born in the *loo*s, the hot summer winds of North India, a voice that speaks to our universal human condition; a poet who speaks to us in a voice as intimate as an eyebrow and as universal as a grandmother.

Thomas McCarthy

From Tushar's Apartment
Malabar Hills, Mumbai

A stable flute pushes me
and a drunken gale retaliates.

My life drifts   like a stranded kite
between the melodious and the mysterious.

Nature gazes like a winsome stranger
strolling   dancing   jumping
like the Bauls of Bengal.

The chirrups of mystic birds
ride on the chariot of the sea
pulled to the shore by its horses.

Thoughts in an intercourse
with naked waves
scream of a world lost in lust.

The hypnotism of the inconclusive
charms me into the grey
of pregnant clouds and pensive waves.

In front of paradoxical nature sounds
I realize
My mind is heavier than my soul.
What seemed impossible
was always possible.

Dear Nature, I wonder
if I should marry you
or keep you as an escort.

The Lost Mango Tree

The mango tree which I reared
is lost today   somewhere
in the jungle of my wishes.

I used to throw whole mangoes
in our backyard
to see them grow up into trees.

Not a single leaf sprouted
except from a half-eaten one.

After watering it   in its infancy
I became engrossed
wining and dining with my life.

After years today
a mangrove in our backyard
shaded my memories
from the hard sun of forgetfulness.

I wish   I had left myself
to the charity of wilderness.

Strange Meetings

Sometimes we run into someone
just for once in our lives

and our bones refuse
to fit inside the skin

the same way.

Plans proceed as waves
and recede as doubts.

A fleeting joy
with gnawing pangs
of apprehension

the stretch between
experience and fear

seems like the time taken by a fish
to reveal and conceal itself

in front of a fish hook.

If I Could

If I were travelling air
without any bony cage,
moral circuits and routes

blowing to the will of paddy fields
smelling the sexual union
of grass roots with wet soil

I would swoop and lift the infant souls
of dead harvested crops

fetching them to their seeds
and allow them to breathe me again.

###

Fears of living
are all entwined
with the lies
we slither into.

Brick by brick
they rise
veiled in the shadows
of our breath

and we leap
like limping grasshoppers
to cross the wall
of illusion.

Aperture

No matter how much you camouflage

some icy words from your slithery tongue
would always reveal you
publicizing your confessions.

More eyes would try to peer
through the aperture you create

for the known seems less
and the unknown inside—vast, virgin.

The world inside must formulate a defence,
for your own words would be used
against you once the aperture widens.

Prepare to shut the door.
No ink on words   no muse on lips
just functional amnesia and secret nostalgia.

Your shadow would pull out of you
and so would the eyes spading your hush.

###

Life becomes a maze
when you have to find
approvals in nos
and disapprovals in yeses

you find there are
boundaries beyond boundaries
thoughts beyond thoughts
lives beyond lives
and
doubts beyond doubts

but no end to end

Masked Eyes

There are eyes behind your vision
from which you cannot escape.

The loneliness of your trembling lips
and the gooseflesh around your nipples

are food for the avowedly innocent trees
leering at your vulnerability.

The winds lick your breath—every gasp

and when you turn around
those eyes are all over you
relishing your longing to be lonely.

You feel the bond   unworldly
for you are caged within bones and blood.

You offered yearning to these eyes.

They would now follow your solitude.

Grandma

The flowers are moving.
She must have whispered
something to them.

The waters are murmuring.
She must have shown them a path.

I lie on my knees
mystified beside her bed
waiting for her to speak
and deliver me from my despair.

The wrinkled skin
pressed against the edge of an old cot
hangs out to touch my forehead.

Grandma is not dead. Her spirit is.

I am being killed by her ennui
and her feeble longing to work again.

Neither am I dying, nor her languor.

Reflections   as skipping stones
are leaping over my melancholy.

Why do I feel my years
getting locked in a second?

Why

Why does life seem
like the skyline impression of an aircraft?

Answer Me, Ma

I still sense your presence
around that door
but a sound from this opening
seems like an echo in the wilderness—

warning as well as bewitching me
to reveal myself to the untravelled.

Still for my senses,
like a deserted impala calf
I am hurling questions and calls
to the woods   drowsy in meditation.

Ma, I know you won't answer.
I am therefore standing

soaking myself
trying to find answers
in the undertone of this rain
falling on the tin house.

In a skirmish with anxiety
I am awake—waiting
to meet sleep in person:
if she has heard you somewhere.

Answer me, Ma.

Or what's the purpose of
perpetuating the thirst of my eyes?

Tears are digging deep inside.

A canyon of remembrances
is getting drilled.

Answer me, Ma.

Slavery of Flags

Through streets
flags fluttered like fans
to give voice to a civilization.

Held by sticks of diplomacy
they struggled like fish
trapped by fish hooks.

Beginnings

When I read a book of poems
I try to think of the moment
when the first flow of thoughts
gushed through its pages.

When I listen to a music album
I try to think of the moment
when the first note
of the first track in it
kissed the muse of its roots.

When I walk barefoot, pressing
ageless soil and gravel,
I try to think of the moment
when the earth was reared from ashes.

But never do they recite
the first anecdote of the planet.

My head   like a shapeless asteroid
revolves around beginnings—

to peer inside
the static stance of time
and the state of mind
that sets it in motion.

Birth of a Hill

Shining through the cracks of life
the warmth of wisdom and resolve

dances like a flaming fire, and then
moves like magma to settle

and solidify   blanketing
a life exposed to harshness

and a hill is born   its rugged allure
hosting the molten inside its womb.

Locked

Sometimes
the iron in a lock
must be thinking
Why was I moulded
into something as such?

A life that came
with boldness
got swept into
isolation—by the tongue
of melancholy rust

hanging like a slave
to the will of the key
and fingers.

Being Yourself

When you feel
like being with yourself
more than with others

life seems
a piece of fiction—

a fallen leaflet
lost in a crowd
of leaves in despair

trying to re-root
itself to the origin
of its birth

and swing in the lap
of its own breath.

Left-Out Love

When realizing the known
seems beyond the bounds of hope
we depend on the unknown.

We no longer remain
a subject of our choices.

Senses heavy with conscience
get buried under
dead drunk fat clouds.

Floating chimeras
and shining instincts
like sunbeams on river skin
start fading out with rains.

Left-out love reigns
as the only gospel.

Hunted

I live in a world
where hunters are often hunted.

The dream to be a Nimrod
gets cornered
by stories from the past
breathed out by breezes

and my vain wish
coughs like an old man.

So I always try to listen to breezes.

They never allow
the hunter in me to grow.

Hence   I am never sought for.
Thus   I won't be ever hunted.

Barely Known

When you say
you barely know someone

close your eyes
and shed all humility inside.

Explore
the validity of your vision
in the darkness
prevailing inside

and then ask

if you could know yourself

and if knowing anyone
adds to knowledge.

Blame

Sometimes some things
don't work out well

and we don't know
whom to blame.

We try to enslave our efforts
with chains of intuition.

We try to entomb destiny
with the nails of blame.

Journeying

by and by life will pass like this
flying like a vagrant kite at night

earlier i used to tour inside my mind
sometimes with my mind into others

then i thought my body should also tour
hence i tour with both of them now

when my bones start forsaking me
i would still tour inside my mind

and count my days of travel
looking at the curve of my shadow

Who Am I?

My obsession to know
who am I
lingers like the sun
setting beneath the wings
of vagrant birds

emerging from nowhere
vanishing into nowhere

When I Hide

Sometimes I hide
by sitting under a tree
allowing its shade
to possess my shadow.

I inhale a dream
of an anonymous cosmos
cuddling a crying infant
in its ever-deepening lap.

My shadow gets lost in its branches
and my emotions fade out
to the rapture of the wild.

Freedom of Love

The sovereignty of love
like free fish
swims in waters
abounding with
drifting fish hooks.

The pain that separates
doesn't care about its repute

for *love* loves
to impale its cutis
to come out
of the cage of survival

the lips clinging
to the truth of detachment

to breathe in a world
without breath.

Cigarette Smoke

The best place to light a cigarette
is beneath a boulevard or a light bulb

and the best way to smoke is
to liberate it towards the light.

You can see your departing breath
falling apart in search of a roof

and then combine towards the light.

Matter sinks into space and then
you are left with ashes.

Life seems a fantastical addiction
as the smell of the finished
seduces you to light another.

When the Wilderness Spoke

My sorrow
looked above
towards the skeleton
of a dead tree
brought to life
by fireflies—playing
and preying around it.

Like a Brick in a Wall

I feel like becoming one
with the walls of this house

staying hidden as one of the bricks
behind cement and paint.

Neither weather nor eyes
would reach me.

By the time the cement sheds off
I would manage to be a part

of some other wall.

The Ferry's Night Horn

Eyes closed, meditating upon
the battering sounds of July rains,

I was reaping my years
with the plough of sentiments.

The soils of echoes from my past
were still loose, vulnerable

and my memories like the Ganges
rolled out images
of ferries in the reddish twilight
touched by the frost of river air.

My eyelids were shut,
listless with exhaustion.
My heartbeats were inspecting the fear
of sensing fossilized days

smiling from within the waters,
their voices mingling with the night horn.

With Time

When I walked
Time passed too fast

and when I ran
it ran faster.

So I stood still
and watched
the evenness in its pace

moving
without any thrust or will
to outstrip me.

Time is my shadow
on the side of light

open to instincts
hidden from naked eyes.

On a Moonlit Night

The moon bathes in the pond
and so does my muse.

The bodyguard palms brood
over it and it shivers   wondering

how to stop the rays
warming the skin of its mistress.

Ripples reveal arousal!

Water sounds from falling
leaves and twigs whisper

of an intercourse
between intangibles.

Parallels

The walls in my room
have been standing for years

looking at each other
but never have they talked
or come together.

Looking at each other

if they try
they would collapse and bleed.

They are like those railway tracks
that shiver holding their plots.

Differences

The only similarity among us is
we are all different

tributaries delving into trenches, jumping out
tasting salt   nearing purpose.

Different names, courses and the ego during flood

get reduced to drops
hanging from deserted taps in summer

or lie as embryos
upon leaves in dewy mornings.

Here is where
the buoyancy of our resemblance unearths.

Infinite thoughts inside finite space

like bubbles drawn to the surface by sunlight.

In a Desert

Scorching heat digs
crevices of pain
in the breathing skin.

Patches of cold air
remind us of rain
and balms

and we survive in hope
gazing at departing streams.

The urge to live

peeping through the edges
of emotion

flies like an ambitious eagle.

Many Faces

When the moon ascends
and wolves step out

roads breathe differently
tucking away their whims
in the blackness of their skin

preying on loneliness
behind the curtain
of insect sounds

and the witnesses
the night birds
sleep during the day
to avoid queries

from a civilization
lying like a broken mirror
with many faces
of the same progress.

Negating the Known

I am finally back on my track
losing the known roads
in which I was ambling till now.

Straight roads always ended in a maze.

I triumphed
in becoming what I am not

and I drifted like

> blind bewilderment loitering
> in an abandoned countryside
>
> haphazard chirping confused as
> soundscapes of perplexity
>
> an overcast crack of dawn
> mistaken as an evenfall
>
> a rapturous love
> abandoned as a mistake.

I am back on my path
from the slavery of the known
to the freedom of the unknown.

In Front of a Burning Corpse

A corpse was burning in the burning ghat by the sea.
A dog was looking at me and whimpering.

Amid the flaming sounds and laughter of waves
the sea seemed to be in gossip with the skies
and the burning corpse looked like an ignited cigar
smoked by the rolling drunk waters.

I felt like an infant ghost   watching its birth.

The tempting body caging the ghost
was leaving a world   which loves to forget.

Breathing seemed as trivial as the cries of the dog
and life was no longer a doubt.

The clouds above were like memories
lurking around the transforming soul.

The flickering sodium lights were trying
to lighten the worth of loving and leaving.

All that was spoken and done
floated like vain lies over untiring waves.

I felt I was someone else
and while battling to become that someone else
I lost myself like a trifling dot in the infinity.

Intentions

Don't blame my intentions.
They can never make or break love.

Your eyes filled with drunkenness
have limited my love to tactility.

It is like sweet waters changing to salty

nearing freedom from their course
realizing the space they deserve.

Your eyes have enthused
my tongue to rear its yearning tip

and your skin has allowed space
to my secret desires.

Tonguing Ashes

A cigarette is changing itself to ashes
in front of my lips.

I have packed my worries
as the tobacco inside
and the soot tastes bitter.

My tolerance is waiting
to reach the filter   to convey to me

the smell of ashes.

Something beyond my convictions
is awaiting to undress itself.

I Never Had a Favourite Face

I remember her fondly
but not her face

her colloquy
but not her eyes

her laughter
but not her lips

her expiration
but not the curve of her breasts.

I never had a favourite face
but a favourite perception.

I gather experiences
like flocking gulls on a shore.

All of them
are not memorable

they don't pull through
the test of surprises.

Slashing and breaking
like waves on stony beaches

a few sensations stay afloat
on the depths of time.

Others drown
tied to the weight of futility.

The Air Around Me

While in class two, I thought of class ten

Now that I have passed so many years
I think of childhood.

I find a familiar air

in every nook and cranny
from alleys to valleys
mountain tents to river boats

packed with responses
about places and passing time

floating in the shallows of quietude
and depths of native smells.

It was there in Tripura, in Ireland...

Now as I was missing the north-east rains
and the chill of Kinsale,
the same air came imbued with petrichor

the same whiff however deep I inhale
                    however deep I introspect

It waits for obscurity   to stop up raptures
and then blows   like a faint whistle

to let me discern
the worth of living so far

and the worth of hoping
in the lap of natural forces.

Reaping the Need to Know

I wonder about the day
I first saw rainfall—

a lost emotion
searching for home

amid thunders
and frog-croons.

My solitary muse
reaping the need to find
the acute rhapsody
in these sinking drops

sat   as a meditating owl
hooting mantras in the zero hour.

No One to Wait at the Doorstep

This door is a forlorn boat of nostalgia.

I could see it from the clay path
leading to my maternal village.
The screeching sounds
of the wooden planks   balancing
upon the still and deep waters of the past
were voices in the wilderness
warning me against stepping into it.

Somewhere on the other side
the smells of bygone days
rode on the shoulders of old strolling breezes
from the last windfall of the village mangrove.
Sleepy summer afternoon sounds
talked me out of smelling them further.

They were all there— moments ago.

The moments have outgrown my hope
and now   as I stand to visit my grandpa

I can hear the *loo**
rushing across a pair of flapping doors
with no one to wait at the doorstep.

*A hot summer wind blowing in North India

Through the Broken Window

This morning   as I stood there
probing my curiosity
I saw new cars and bikes
passing by the window.

Morning prayers
from a new kindergarten
could be heard   and loud debates
in newly opened shops
seemed more factual
than befuddled newspapers

but not a single face was known
not a single voice was familiar.

Just above my eyebrows
on the wall behind
a new crack was born.
I could see it shivering in the panes.

A weird gloom and sporadic frustration
led me to this window today

where memories have no houses to reside in
and time is too restless to settle.

The Rooftop

The rooftop of my 1997 house
is my daily haunt in the dead of night.
It is a quotidian habit of my solitude
that embarks upon the cries of foxes
and euphonious breezes
blowing from wheezing trees.

Sometimes the bravery of facing life
seems to be a pretence
and this daily part of my life on the rooftop
acts as a respite from weariness
and a route to escape.

Occasionally an owl sits in the roadside mahogany
shooting me with cryptic jargon—
which I prefer to the day's cacophony.

An unquenched thirst smiles
at the forewarning clouds.

My thoughts have sucked the veins
of innovation and reconstruction
leaving me to my bones and flesh.

A foolhardy life is straining to walk free
from the wraps of cocoons interlaced by time.

Dadaji

The birds were returning home
in the backdrop of an amber sky.
Some kites were circling
above their newly built eyries.
My house has always been a landmark
for whom the whole sky was one path.

Watching them yesterday
from a caged balcony—
I was thinking of my Dadaji*.
His image   clear enough
to lead me through forests
                    through stories   surprises.

I had a strange joy in my infancy
sitting in hutments with him
throughout harvest
overlooking lush paddies   awaiting
the clean sunny smell of stacked hay.

Today morning
Dadaji visited me   uninformed.

Leaving the doorstep
he held me by my shoulders—
You aren't that little child anymore
you won't come running behind...

I stood bidding adieu.
He smiled   still aesthetic in his nineties.

Above, birds flew in an ultramarine sky
to start their day. We are the same but
our priorities have shifted their course.

*Grandfather in Hindi

Through the Specs of an Old Man

An old man was standing frivolously
in front of that eerie mansion
we have always been warned of.
The eldritch sounds   during the nights of infancy
were believed to descend from there.

Standing behind him   endeavouring to peep
through his thick glasses
I tried to gauge the relation
between his fidgety eyes and embattled lips

that were releasing glib phrases
into the surrounding air.

The mansion and its days   have drifted apart.
Creepers are rebuilding an abode
through the fissures of age.
Banana herbs are celebrating
with wild flowers and bougainvilleas
on the edges of a fountain   given away
on the verge of a silent death.

The old man turned and smiled—
his glance   framing his rounded lips
was like the mansion itself
personified into a sudden happiness.

The walls   once eerie
were now a residue of remembrances
peeping through his thick specs.

Some Things Are Best Unchanged

While loitering   in the glassy arcades
of a mall in Dubai   I WhatsApped Ma a selfie.
It was meant to commission   the little joy
I was able to unearth in these sheeny shops.

There was no reply
except a phone call   asking me to stay well.

This morning   as I travelled home
the green fields and huts sprawled
in front of my eyes.

I brooded   like those leaning date palms
musing over   their recumbent reflections
in the village pond.

April and My Plastic Sunflowers

The four plastic sunflowers in my bedroom—
the way they swayed in the ceiling fan's air
were the functional year-long April for me.

The fallen twigs of a meditating winter
and the deadwood sanity of their roughness,
the begging deserts of the patient summer
and the coarseness of their ravaged mirages,
the thin tune of the homesick autumn
and the restlessness of their alcoholic breezes
were never like fresh seasonal fruits to me,
for I had the functional year-long April in my bedroom:
those four plastic sunflowers.

It hasn't been long that my wedding and divorce
both in their infancy
ended the perpetual April in my room
by demanding those yellow sunflowers
in the package of reparation.

It was four seasons ago and the spring of April
now seems a creepy plastic serpent
irresistibly insidious in its illusory cruelty
as my new girlfriend from the same city
talked of bringing new plastic flowers into my room.

My Chained Faith

The far-flung whistle of the colliery
and of the Calcutta Mail
calls me every day after dinner.

The train's shrill echo
and the rhythmic melody of the wheels
form a sublime image
of the girl out of my dreams

waving and smiling
screaming and crying
standing and waiting
just for me amid grasses,
trees and hedges that wave
in solitude and hope.

The curvature of the lopsided land
plays hide-and-seek
with the clouds and the moon
blurring realism.

My belief is incurable and so is
the façade of pleasure that I show
while I compellingly follow
the whistle of the colliery.

My faith lies in the train,
in the wilderness
and the vaporous figure of my love
while my whims are chained
to famine and society
that may think me mad
once I leave my job and run
into the hazy backwoods.

Inception or Epilogue?

Over and over again
I was putting my drowsy head back
on the neck-rest   as my driver sped
scraping the car through a jungle road.

My eyelids   unlatched by the jolts
located an endless territory of trees
waving towards an isolated light—
showing up a path
that starts and ends in itself.

Thick trunks   twisting off their weariness
imparted songs of faith.
Expansive fields   engaged in rapt gossip
with the skies   removed the curtain of clouds.

The birds were silent—
No chirrup.   No fluttering of wings.
They were stuck inside a web of hypnosis
stretched out by a mystical symphony.

And I moved as a trespasser   with faith
in the breathing canvas of silhouettes.

The alluring light in a distance
burnt as embers in a fireplace.

The world was within me
and I was everywhere outside.

We Deserve a Jungle

Every time I fall intoxicated
I try to visualize the world
as a rainforest—drowsy
and drunk with tranquility
cushioned amid creepers
vaguely painted by
hallucinating artists.

No languages, no debates

Just disparate sounds
and occasional shrieks
intruding a deep slumber
in the backdrop
of dimly lit mosses.

We are worthy
of being in a jungle
both as free beings
and as those who have
jailed their own existence
in the cells
of work and weariness.

We deserve to be on a par
with animals and insects.

A Duck's Life

Those who keep searching for
the meaning of life are not born yet.
They might take a bite of unfamiliar lifestyles.
They might look out for a pond
and watch a domestic duck's life—

How it ducks every difficulty
floating and dipping its head
in the same waters every day.

How it manages a life
from home to pond
through hedges and marshes
easing the earth off its own weight
by just floating—floating with a mind
that grows old without realizing.

How it paddles through the waters
of time, and shakes them off
with a joyful flutter of wings.

Looking at Lake Ohrid*

In front of the silent vastness
of seas and mountains
my speech is lost somewhere
between my eyes and my breath.

The countless lines in my palms
flow like rivers into the unending.

I see a serene blue sky   mating
with a blue lake   in the floor of my eyes.

With all my frailties and potency
I trust   I exist today   as a child
of sky and water.

I feel my existence isn't untrue.

Every snowcapped mountain
every underwater cave
every movement of fish
makes me live a new life
every moment I stand here.

In just one dive into the winds
I feel   all the riddles of my life are solved

and all my unnamed expectations
have come to life   somewhere here
between my eyes and my breath.

*A lake in Macedonia

Afloat in Darkness

Once drawn into blackness and desolation
light will always be a fallacy.

Still, daylight, lamplight, firelight and
all types of glow would beguile you
making you proceed obdurately
towards the mistaken source of light.

By the time darkness reappears
the sundown will help you apprehend—
light is just a flicker   drifting in darkness.

There is no end   and there was no genesis.

Teach Me

I wish there were lessons on

how to regret
how to unite words
and how to embrace
a shooting anxiety.

I wish   I had a tutor
to teach me

about the tangled alliance
between human emotions
and states of being

if living alone
has something to do with solitude.

Liberty of Half-Dead Creations

With dry foliage
all over my backyard
I yelled to the mahogany
drooling over our boundary wall:
Comb your hairs once a week.
Time is more kind to you.
You have an adequacy
of years to avow your claims.

Each time I shouted,
it would drop another
leaf on me.

Most of them
half-dead
carried an echo
of a poet's life
rooted to a room
where his tired poems
would rather lie
on a shabby couch
than walk towards freedom.

Half-dead poems:
they must draw impulse
from the fallen leaves.

Detached from
their deep-rooted creator
these leaves seem
to enjoy more liberty
as they grin
through bare veins

free to walk
without a canopy
without a daily craving
to be nurtured.

Stories Told by Dimness

In a smoky evening
a dim light calmed me
by telling stories about my life—
stories hidden
from my eyes and ears.

The years didn't pass in a second.
I didn't grow up on my own.

There are untold tales
etched in the untouched walls
of my childhood.
There are projected designs
of my upbringing
in the winds   which I didn't breathe.

Today dimness has a pact with them
to tell me
how and where I exist

to allow me enough time
to think over my existence
before it is finally blown out.

The Homeless

Split bolster, tattered shoes,
a lean bed sheet—

the ménage of the homeless
sleeps together.

He keeps mumbling
to them and asserts

I don't seek charity—

but someone to chat with

for my ossified abilities
to grip sunshine.

Talaq Talaq Talaq

To the women who stood against Triple Talaq

When days turned dusky for you
I knew you waited for the full moon

to see how *baya* weavers rub beaks
in consent to preserve their love.

Like a globetrotter who never rides
on the fanfare of trumpets—of war and glory

I knew how you craved for equity
crying like a Stradivarius.

Your nikah was no devotion,
but the carousal of a ravenous brute

and as you realized those owls
waiting to carry your chicks

like pouches of field mice
all that you prayed for was a new moon.

I know now, from your palms
sliding from ears to cheeks

and from your eyelids
opening like hushed oyster shells—

pearls still shine in your eyes
that never feared, never gave up

screaming a hundred talaqs
to *talaq, talaq, talaq*

Tears

We were born artless, but we mastered the art of hating
when we felt the need to classify tears.

Nobody Speaks of You, Syria

You have shrunk to a handful of wet dust—
wet from tears and rapacious semen.

The heralds look at you as a whore

and your screams have no walls
to enclose their echoes. All have fallen.

Your ovaries are dead.
Your ribs have turned into razors
wiping out your sentiments.

The bullets you have consumed
have rusted inside your womb
and stained the colour of your blood.

Civilization looks
as blank as a dry river
that doesn't thirst for rain.

Somewhere in your ruins
hope peeps like a thief
through the broken tooth
of a child smiling at a broken tank.

Through her eyes

you look so lean, Syria,
but your history is getting fat.

The Soldier in the Moss

The moss of the trunk   through its chroma
has been trying to rot a body—hosting a soldier's
dead wishes   clamped to an obstinate belief.

The the soldier's boot   is still trying to step out.
Its rugged skin hangs out from its wounded tip
either in search of his gun   chained by red rust
or for the pages of his diary   hidden in foliage.

Deep down the depths of the mist   I left
a sniper   to let him find out the worth of war
in the quest of peace—how machines have evolved
from his *gewehr*   to my long-neck killer.

Hairless   like an atheist monk   the skeleton-tree sat
in blasphemous meditation   with the moss dead set on
to tinge the vainness of valour   with vapours and earth.

Snapshots of a Dying Soldier

1.

A reluctant combat helmet   lying over a weary head
and an ever-vigilant gun   pregnant with bullets
lean against each other in moot discipline.
A mixture of the absurd and the fantastic.

2.

Eyes fixed on a rising dawn   with the sun at heart
absorb drowsy silhouettes and weeping clouds.
They blink like *Mimosa pudicas*   as thoughts perish
on the borderline of infused patriotism.

3.

A shroud of smoke   follows far-flung air strikes
and the cloud above roars   to obliterate screaming pleas
A tired imagination rises   and falls like musical notes
on the strings of realism boxed inside solitude.

4.

A faithless hand burns a cigarette   and pelts stones
at a nearby ditch   frowning at the obvious.
A pair of embattled lips murmurs childhood songs.
An ominous twister forming from wandering smokes.

5.

The head lies flat   with dreaming eyes fixed at dawn.
The gun awaits its next partner   and the helmet escapes.
The feeble ditch   almost dry   refuses to lend water
and the seeping blood refuses   to lend it either.

6.

A family in its infancy   plays at home   uninformed.
Reasons scratch against broken walls   to find ways
of banishing the magical gun   from the pop culture of war.

To Syrian Children

You all are culpable—for wending your way to schools,
for going to hospitals, for playing in open spaces and
for keeping at your dreams within a country in rags.

Yes, you never knew—you would be going down
with a fever that would burn your flesh into a universal
white fume—blooming in newspapers.

But liven up the carcasses now. You wanted to be
in suits like Putin or Trump. Look what have you ended
up with—

the sweat of literate talks in a ground of experimentation.

The handsome presidents have osculated you a goodbye.

Now burn yourselves completely, or they would light cigarettes
out of you—blaming you for the cancer rampant in the air.

Don't let yourselves be counted—history will be framed
without you.

Vanish with the fumes and transform into water.

It would fulfill
    your hope of staying away from fire
    and your desire to wash blind eyes.

Unborn Ones, please retreat to your mothers' wombs.
The guns are booming outside.
Wait till they have the ear to celebrate your first cry.

Death of a Dalit

The muddy clouds on top
are toiling to get sieved.
The colander is heavy with mud,
years of dilapidation
clogging its pores.

Thunder is trying
to take us far afield
from the subject at hand—
the final exit of that boy—
a life that could have been ours.

Every so often a brisk current of air
veering through the heart
warns of an incoming cloudburst.

A collapse of the system
is in the offing.

The Ragpicker

It was amazing how
the little girl came
to me and asked
for a coin.

The world is
throwing less waste,
it seems.

Earlier ragpickers
were reticent
or perhaps I am
a dustbin
of riches now.

Faith in Times of War

A summer wars inside
and tears retire

like defeated soldiers banished
from the duchy of blood.

Wounded muses scorn death
in corners of daily roads
like unabating smoke
from half-burnt cigarettes.

Blowing blues
beset with the malignancy of missiles
clamour against rusted apertures.

The tentacles of faith
propagate hope to survivors
and the surprise of explosions
dusts it off.

The air smells of poison
and a vacuum surges.

Still   we breathe   deep in faith
for we were born out of love
and will be buried in warmth.

Haze and High

The sky looks clear.
Still I can't see through it.

The depth of the clear
seems unclear.

The distance of my insight
hovers like a severed kite

unable to use its freedom.

Anticipations Grip Back

Arabian Nights, Denver, The Four Brothers
and a lonely quivering glass of whisky

curing the sores of wistfulness
emerging from the breeze of a dry winter

lurk like the ghostly hissing
of dry foliage in icy midnights.

Untitled

The less I sense
the less bitter
it tastes—

walking a globe
with countless eyes.

I wish to be the soil
of the boundary

begging for lines
to survive

and shed off my ears
to the moments shaping scars

as facts arrive
veiled in versions.

Smells

The nose digs up tales
buried under the humus
of our recollections.

Without sight
smells dig deep
inside our psyche
chiselling the moss
around our subconscious

and what was lost reveals itself
like a breeze
on the edge
of a world without light

where air is the book of sojourns
and the nose the reader.

Asides

When I die
you would wonder
about the time
I was dying.

ii

Sometimes you cross a road
without knowing
and then you know
it was there.

iii

When old leaves fall
trees celebrate the space
for the new.

iv

When I am here
there is a world locked inside me.
And when I am gone
my world would roam the earth.

More from our mint

Author of WAYS OF SEEING and
Winner of the Booker Prize for G

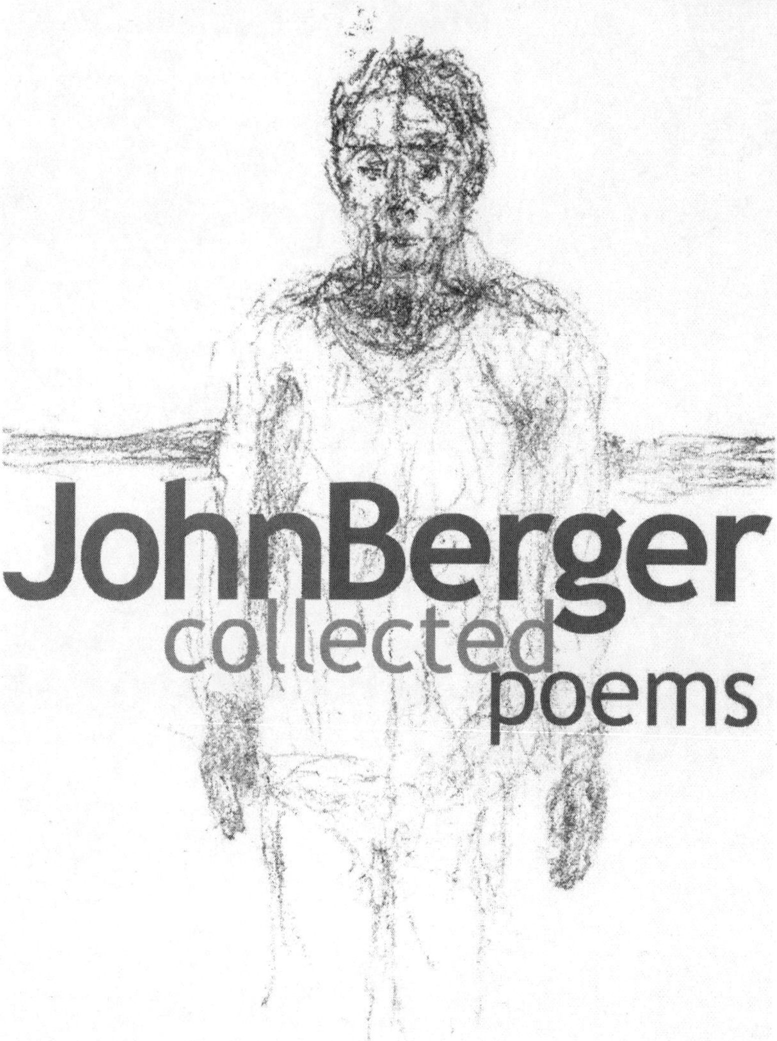

JohnBerger

collected poems

Manohar Shetty
Creatures
Great and Small
POEMS

Manohar Shetty
Morning
Light

Heart's Beast
NEW AND SELECTED POEMS
Saleem Peeradina

SOPHIA NAZ
Pointillism

Rochelle Potkar
Paper Asylum